Keto Sl

Cookbook for Delicious and Easy Ketogenic Cooking
Low Carb Healthy Recipes for Your Crockpot to Lose Weight Fast

OLIVIA STRATTON

Stir Fried Beef with Veggies **41**

Cheesy Beef Casserole **43**

Keto Irish Beef Stew **45**

Broccoli Beef Soup **47**

Superb Ground Beef Keto Style **49**

Vegetarian

Broccoli and Tofu Curry **51**

Minestrone Soup **53**

Kale Quiche **55**

Vegan Frittata with Feta and Artichoke Hearts **57**

Spinach Stuffed Portobello **59**

Herbed Vegetable Soup **61**

Cauliflower Pizza with Low Carb Alfredo Sauce **63**

Seafood

Poached Salmon **65**

Cod and Vegetables **67**

Veggie Shrimps **69**

Fish Stock **71**

Pollock Stew **73**

Trout & Broccoli Chowder 75

Garlic Shrimp 77

Seafood Scampi 79

Desserts

Lemon Cake 81

Low Carb Apple Bread 83

Chocolate Chip Zucchini Bread 85

Keto Mocha Fudge Cake 87

Cranberry Walnut Bars 89

Berry Sauce 91

Ketogenic Diet Tips

1. You need to stay hydrated all the time

Specialists recommend drinking 30 oz of water in the first hour once you wake up and add another 30-46 oz of water before noon time. In order to stay properly hydrated you should be drinking at least 100-120 ounces of water on a daily basis.

2. Exercise regularly

Regular resistance training exercises along with running and low-intensity exercise help to balance the level of sugar in blood and improve the ability to get into and maintain ketosis.

3. Practice intermittent fasting

If you want to get yourself into ketosis and maintain it, intermittent fasting will be the best option for you, as with intermittent fasting you will reduce calories and stop consummation of protein or carbs. However, it is strongly recommended to start consuming low quantities of carbs for at least couple of days before starting intermittent fasting as not to get a hypoglycemic episode.

4. Wisely choose carbs that you consume

Ketogenic diet is a low-carb diet and it is recommended to consume nutrient rich carbohydrate sources such as non-starchy veggies and small amounts of low-glycemic fruits.

5. Use MCT oil wherever you can

Consumption of high quality medium chain triglyceride (MCT) oil will allow you to consume more protein/carbs and maintain ketosis. Doing this is probably the best thing you can do to actually get into ketosis and maintain it.

6. Keep stress as low as possible

Stress shuts down the ability to maintain the ketosis. If you are stressing a lot, maybe you should reset your goal to simply stay on a lower carb, anti-inflammatory diet for some time.

7. Get enough sleep

If you do not get enough sleep or the quality of your sleep is poor, you will not be able to get into and maintain the ketosis. Thus, make sure you do sleep well and enough.

Slow Cooker Useful Tips

1. Start with carefully reading the instructions for your device

Every slow cooker comes with a manual that you should carefully study, as it contains terms of use, additional useful tips, and, most importantly, information on how use it safely.

2. Try not to open the lid often

Every time you open the lid to check or to stir the dish it adds 15 to 20 minutes of cooking time. Most recipes in this book do not require stirring at all, so just close the lid and wait till the cooking time is up.

3. Thaw your food

Do not load your slow cooker with icy ingredients (unless it is prepackaged slow cooker meal) as it may create perfect conditions for bacteria flourish. Thaw vegetables and meat before cooking in your slow cooker.

4. Take care of your slow cooker

Make sure you keep the ceramic insert of your slow cooker from temperature difference. If you store the Crockpot insert with food in a refrigerator, let it cool down to room temperature first. Also put the hot insert on a dishtowel first and not on a cold counter.

5. Do not overcrowd your slow cooker

If you cook whole chicken or big roasts, make sure you have a suitable Crockpot size. It is recommended to fill a slow cooker not more than two-thirds full.

6. Brown your food first

If you want to boost your dish flavor, you can just brown the food a bit before transferring it to a slow cooker. This allows you to get an additional caramelized flavor

Za'atar Chicken

Servings: 4
Cooking time: 3-6 hours

Ingredients

    3 tablespoons olive oil
    2 ½ tablespoons lemon zest
    3 teaspoons garlic, minced
    ¼ cup za'atar herbs
    ½ cup lemon juice
    1 1/3 teaspoons kosher salt
    8 chicken 6 to 8 oz thighs, skinless
    2 lemons, cut in 4 wedges
    2 green onions bunches, with ends chopped

Instructions

1. Mix olive oil and za'atar herbs in a bowl, add salt and lemon zest. Add the chicken and coat to cover.
2. Add olive oil to the slow cooker. Put the chicken into slow cooker, add lemons and garlic.
3. Close the lid and cook on Low for 6 hours or on High for 3 hours.
4. Serve topped with green onions.

Nutritional info

Calories: 438
Fats (g): 35
Net carbs (g): 2.7
Protein (g): 19.1

Slow Cooker Chicken Vesuvio

Servings: 6
Cooking time: 3-7 hours

Ingredients

    1 whole chicken, divided into parts
    2 tablespoons butter, unsalted
    1 cauliflower head, cut in florets
    1 sprig fresh oregano
    8 garlic cloves
    1 teaspoon dried thyme
    ¼ cup dry white wine
    ½ cup chicken broth
    1 teaspoon black pepper
    1 cup snow peas (optional)
    2 tablespoons olive oil
    salt, to taste
    parsley

Instructions

1. Season chicken with salt and pepper.
2. Mix wine, broth, oregano and butter in a bowl.
3. Add olive oil into slow cooker. Put chicken, cauliflower, garlic and peas into the Crockpot, pour wine mixture over it.
4. Close the lid and cook on Low for 7 hours or on High for 3 hours.
5. Serve topped with parsley.

Nutritional info

Calories: 204
Fats (g): 22.3
Net carbs (g): 5.4
Protein (g): 16

Dijon Chicken

Servings: 3
Cooking time: 4-6 hours

Ingredients
>   3 skinless, boneless chicken breast
>   1 onion, thinly sliced
>   2 garlic cloves, finely chopped
>   1 cup chicken broth
>   ½ cup lemon juice
>   1 tablespoon lemon zest
>   3 tablespoons Dijon mustard
>   2 teaspoons dried oregano
>   1 teaspoon salt
>   ½ teaspoon ground black pepper

Instructions
1. Season chicken with salt, pepper and oregano.
2. Put chicken into slow cooker and layer onion over it.
3. Mix broth, mustard, lemon juice and zest in a separate bowl.

4. Pour the mixture over chicken. Cook on Low for 6 hours or for 4 hours on High.

Nutritional info
Calories: 196
Fats (g): 25.6
Net carbs (g): 7.3
Protein (g): 18.4

Chicken Burgers

Servings: 5
Cooking time: 3-5 hours

Ingredients

1.5 lb ground chicken
½ small onion, minced
1 teaspoon dried sage
1 egg
salt and pepper, to taste
2 tablespoon butter
½ cup water
almond meal if needed

Instructions

1. Mix ground chicken, onion, sage, egg, water, salt and pepper in a big bowl. Add almond meal if there is extra liquid in a mixture.
2. Form medium sized patties, about 1 inch thick.
3. Melt butter in a slow cooker, put chicken patties there. Make sure there is enough space between them.
4. Close the lid and cook on Low for 5 hours or on High for 3 hours. The patties should be firm.
5. Serve on buns with vegetables or desired toppings.

Nutritional info

Calories: 315
Fats (g): 25.6
Net carbs (g): 0.8
Protein (g): 14.6

Lemon Marinade Chicken

Servings: 2
Cooking time: 6-8 hours

Ingredients
  juice of 1 lemon
  2 cloves garlic, minced
  2 tablespoons olive oil
  1 tablespoon black pepper
  2 chicken breasts, skinless and boneless
  salt, to taste

Instructions
1. Mix olive oil, garlic, lemon juice and pepper in a bowl with a fork.
2. Put the chicken breast into the slow cooker and pour the mixture over the chicken.
3. Cook on high with the lid closed for 6 hours or on low for 8 hours.
4. Enjoy your meal.

Nutritional info
Calories: 402
Fats (g): 35.5
Net carbs (g): 4.1
Protein (g): 15.7

Chicken & Bean Stew

Servings: 4
Cooking time: 4-6 hours

Ingredients

 4 tablespoons olive oil
 1 big onion, chopped
 6 strips smoked streaky bacon, chopped
 8 chicken legs or thighs, skin removed
 1 tablespoon smoked paprika
 2 cans diced tomatoes and garlic
 1 tablespoon dried oregano or mixture of dried
 herbs
 2 cans black soy beans
 salt and pepper to taste
 7 oz water
 cheddar cheese, grated

low carb tortilla chips

For Low Carb Sauce:
> 2 oz apple cider vinegar
> 4 oz water
> 2 tablespoons butter
> 1 can tomato paste
> 1 teaspoon onion powder
> 2 teaspoons pepper
> 1 teaspoon Worcestershire sauce
> ½ teaspoon Liquid Smoke Sauce
> salt, to taste

Instructions

1. Cook the sauce first: mix all the sauce ingredients in a saucepan and bring to a boil over high heat.
2. Turn the heat down to low and simmer for 1 hour while stirring from time to time. Let the sauce cool down and refrigerate.
3. Preheat oil in a slow cooker skillet with the lid closed.
4. Add sliced onions and bacon, cook on High with the lid closed for 1 hour until the onions are soft and slightly browned, the bacon should be crunchy.
5. Put the chicken parts into slow cooker.
6. Add tomatoes, herbs, paprika, sauce, salt, pepper and water.
7. Add beans, close the lid and cook on High for 3-4 hours or on Low for 6 hours, stir occasionally.

8. Check if the chicken is soft. If it is not cover the cooker once again and boil for another 15 minutes.
9. Serve topped with cheddar and tortilla chips.

Nutritional info

Calories: 328
Fats (g): 38
Net carbs (g): 9.8
Protein (g): 20

Chicken Breast & Zucchini Salad

Servings: 3
Cooking time: 6 hours

Ingredients

¼ cup olive oil
1 lb boneless, skinless chicken breasts
11 oz zucchini, thinly sliced
¼ cup fresh lemon juice
½ red onion, thinly sliced
coarse salt and ground pepper, to taste
¼ cup chopped pecans
1 bunch (about 8 oz) spinach, chopped
¼ cup Parmesan cheese, grated
¼ cup fresh mint, chopped

Instructions

1. Mix lemon juice, ¼ cup oil, pepper and salt in a bowl.
2. Season zucchini with the mixture.

3. Put some oil to the slow cooker and put chicken into it. Add seasoned zucchini, onion, spinach and mint.
4. Cook on Low for 6 hours.
5. Once cooked add pecans and parmesan cheese.

Nutritional info
Calories: 321
Fats (g): 42.3
Net carbs (g): 12.1
Protein (g): 31.3

Roasted Chicken

Servings: 6
Cooking time: 5 hour 40 minutes

Ingredients
1 (4 lb) chicken
1 bulb fennel, tops removed, cut into wedges
1 yellow onion, thickly sliced
1 bunch fresh thyme, plus 20 sprigs
1 carrot, cut into 2-inch chunks (optional)
freshly ground black pepper
2 lemons, cut into halves
1 head garlic, cut in half crosswise
3 tablespoons butter, melted
2 tablespoons olive oil
salt to taste

Instructions
1. Rinse the chicken and tap dry with a paper towel. Season the chicken with salt and pepper, rub it with garlic and pour butter over it.

25

2. Stuff the chicken with thyme, garlic, and lemon.
3. Put onions, fennel, and carrots into slow cooker. Season with salt and pepper, add olive oil.
4. Place the chicken on top of vegetables.
5. Close the lid and cook the chicken on Low for 6 hours.
6. Remove the chicken and put it into a baking dish. Preheat the oven to 350 F and cook the chicken in the oven for 4-5 minutes.
7. Slice the chicken and serve with vegetables.

Nutritional info
Calories: 495
Fats (g): 26.1
Net carbs (g): 8.3
Protein (g): 16

Chicken Noodle Soup

Servings: 4
Cooking time: 4-7 hours

Ingredients

½ onion, chopped
½ carrot, thinly sliced
1 garlic clove, minced
8 cups water
2 small chicken breasts
2 bay leaves
1 package cooked Tofu Shirataki noodles, drained and rinsed
salt, pepper, to taste

Instructions

1. In a slow cooker mix water, carrot, onion, garlic, bay leaves, salt and pepper.
2. Add chicken breasts to a slow cooker.
3. Close the lid and cook on Low for 6 hours or on High for 3 hours.

4. Once cooked, remove chicken breasts and shred. Remove bay leaves.
5. Add noodles to the slow cooker and cook for 30 minutes on Low with the lid closed.
6. Skim fat from the soup and serve hot.

Nutritional info
Calories: 149
Fats (g): 29
Net carbs (g): 3.3
Protein (g): 19.9

Chicken Salad with Celery and Pecans

Servings: 4
Cooking time: 3 hours

Ingredients
    2 chicken breasts
    ½ cup water
    ½ onion, diced
    2 ribs celery, diced
    ½ cup pecans, chopped
For Keto Mayo
    1 egg yolk
    ½ teaspoon Dijon mustard
    2 teaspoons lemon juice
    ½ teaspoon white wine vinegar
    10 tablespoons avocado oil
    1/2 teaspoon salt

Instructions

1. Put chicken, onion, celery and water into a slow cooker. Cook for 3 hours on Low until chicken is cooked.
2. Shred the chicken and drain vegetables. Cool them to room temperature.
3. Meanwhile blend all mayo ingredients in a food processor (for about 30 seconds). The mixture should become lighter and thicker.
4. Slowly add avocado oil to the mixture while blending constantly.
5. Now mix the chicken, vegetables, pecans and mayo in a bowl.
6. Serve separately or with main course.

Nutritional info

Calories: 276
Fats (g): 28.4
Net carbs (g): 5.6
Protein (g): 13.6

Chicken with Thai Peanut Sauce

Servings: 4
Cooking time: 3-6 hours

Ingredients

4 boneless chicken thighs, cut into bite size pieces
½ cup canned coconut milk
½ cup unsweetened peanut butter
3 tablespoons toasted sesame oil
2 tablespoons soy sauce
1 tablespoons lime juice
1 garlic clove, minced
1 teaspoon powdered ginger
2 tablespoons peanuts, chopped
fresh cilantro

Instructions

1. Put chicken thighs into a slow cooker.
2. Mix coconut milk, peanut butter, garlic, soy sauce and lime juice in a medium bowl.
3. Pour the mixture over chicken. Add some water if the sauce is too thick.
4. Close the lid and cook on Low for 6 hours or on High for 3 hours.
5. You may cut the chicken into pieces and return to the sauce to marinate even better.
6. Serve chicken with spaghetti squash or with salad topped with peanuts and cilantro.

Nutritional info

Calories: 480
Fats (g): 40.6
Net carbs (g): 6
Protein (g): 24

Pumpkin Turkey Chili

Servings: 3
Cooking time: 3 hours

Ingredients
- 1 ½ cups fresh pumpkin, cubed
- 1 can black soy beans
- 1 tablespoon olive oil
- 1 tablespoon chili powder
- 1 ½ tablespoons brown sugar substitute
- 1 onion, chopped
- 2 lb ground turkey
- 1 can (20 oz) diced tomatoes
- 1 tablespoon pumpkin pie spice

Instructions
1. Preheat olive oil in a pan over low heat for 3 minutes. Add turkey and stir for 7-8 minutes, drain fat.
2. Transfer turkey into the slow cooker and add beans, pumpkin, chili powder, pumpkin pie spice, sugar, diced tomatoes and onion.

3. Cook on High for 3 hours with the lid closed.

Nutritional info
Calories: 300
Fats (g): 42.1
Net carbs (g): 11.7
Protein (g): 21.9

Turkey Breasts

Servings: 2
Cooking time: 5-8 hours

Ingredients

4 skinless, boneless turkey breasts
2 garlic cloves, minced
5 bay leaves
2 tablespoons onion powder
1 teaspoon dried oregano
salt and black pepper, to taste
2 cups chicken broth

Instructions

1. Season turkey breasts with salt, pepper, oregano and onion powder.
2. Put the turkey into a slow cooker.
3. Pour broth into a slow cooker; make sure you do not wash off the turkey seasoning.
4. Add garlic and sage leaves.

5. Cook on Low for 8 hours or on High for 1 hour and then on Low for 5 hours.

Nutritional info
Calories: 352
Fats (g): 29.6
Net carbs (g): 5.9
Protein (g): 14

Beef Filled Lettuce Wraps

Servings: 3
Cooking time: 3 hours 15 minutes

Ingredients

  1 lb ground beef
  2 teaspoons olive oil
  2 scallions, chopped
  2 inch piece ginger, grated
  ¼ cup chopped peanuts
  2 cloves garlic, minced
  1 head lettuce leaves, separated, cleaned and dried
  1 teaspoon red pepper flakes
  ¼ cup sriracha sauce
  salt and freshly ground black pepper, to taste
  2 tablespoons soy sauce

Instructions

1. Preheat oil in a pan and add beef. Cook for 5 minutes stirring and drain the grease.

2. Preheat oil in a slow cooker skillet with the lid closed and then add cooked beef.
3. Add garlic, ginger, soy sauce, scallions, sriracha and red pepper flakes, stir well.
4. Cook on Low for 2-3 hours until brown.
5. Once cooked add peanuts and season with pepper and salt.
6. Serve wrapped in lettuce leaves.

Nutritional info

Calories: 411
Fats (g): 28.9
Net carbs (g): 8.9
Protein (g): 20.9

Meatballs with Spinach

Servings: 4
Cooking time: 6 hours

Ingredients
   1 lb. ground beef
   1 (10 oz) package frozen spinach
   ¼ cup parmesan cheese, grated
   4 cups chicken or beef bone broth
   1/8 teaspoon ground black pepper
   salt, to taste

Instructions
   1. Mix cheese, salt, pepper, beef, and stir to combine.
   2. Roll the mixture into small meatballs.
   3. Put meatballs into the slow cooker, add broth, spinach and cook on low for 6 hours.
   4. Remove from the heat and sprinkle with additional cheese (optional). Check for seasoning.

Nutritional info
Calories: 484
Fats (g): 38.2
Net carbs (g): 3.1
Protein (g): 27.3

Stir Fried Beef with Veggies

Servings: 3
Cooking time: 3-6 hours

Ingredients

 1 lb beef sirloin, cut into 1 ½-inch strips
 2 tablespoons sesame seeds, toasted
 1½ cups fresh broccoli florets
 1 carrot, thinly sliced
 1 onion, chopped
 2 garlic cloves, minced
 1 red bell pepper, cut into strips
For Sauce:
 ¼ cup water
 ¼ cup coconut aminos or soy sauce
 2 tablespoons white vinegar

1 teaspoon toasted evoo
1 tablespoon ginger
1 teaspoon honey

Instructions
1. Put beef, broccoli florets, carrots, onion, bell pepper and garlic into slow cooker.
2. Mix water, aminos or soy sauce, vinegar, evoo, ginger and honey in a medium bowl.
3. Pour sauce over beef and vegetables.
4. Close the lid and cook on Low for 6 hours or on High for 3 hours.
5. Season with sesame seeds once cooked. Serve with pasta or rice.

Nutritional info
Calories: 477
Fats (g): 31.5
Net carbs (g): 9.5
Protein (g): 28.6

Cheesy Beef Casserole

Servings: 6
Cooking time: 3-6 hours

Ingredients

1.5 lbs lean ground beef
2 teaspoons olive oil
1 tablespoon garlic, minced
1 tablespoon tomato paste (can be substituted
with tomato puree of 1-2 tomatoes)
1 onion, chopped
2 cups grated cheddar cheese
1 cup low fat cottage cheese
¾ cup heavy cream
2 cups water
salt, pepper, to taste

Instructions

1. Heat oil in a medium pan over high heat. Add ground beef and sauté for 5 minutes. Drain fat and set aside.
2. Clean the pan and heat some more oil in it, add onions and cook for 3 minutes. Add garlic and cook for 30 seconds.
3. Put beef, onion and garlic into a slow cooker. Add water, tomato paste, salt and pepper. Mix well.
4. Close the lid and cook on Low for 6 hours or on High for 3 hours.
5. Open the lid, add cheddar and cottage cheese, heavy cream and stir gently. Close the lid and cook on Low for another 1 hour until the cheese is melted.

Nutritional info

Calories: 473
Fats (g): 27.4
Net carbs (g): 4.9
Protein (g): 49.7

Keto Irish Beef Stew

Servings: 4
Cooking time: 3-6 hours

Ingredients

    1 lb beef stew meat, cut into 1-inch pieces
    2 tablespoons coconut oil
    1 onion, chopped
    1 carrot, chopped
    1 parsnip, chopped
    2 oz mushrooms, halved
    4 cloves garlic, chopped
    ½ teaspoon thyme
    2 bay leaves
    2 teaspoon Worcestershire sauce
    1 cup Guinness stout

1 cup beef stock
1 teaspoon dried oregano
fresh parsley
salt and pepper, to taste

Instructions

1. Heat oil in a big skillet over medium heat, add beef. Cook for 5-10 minutes stirring constantly until beef is browned from all sides.
2. Transfer beef to a slow cooker.
3. Add onion, carrot, parsnip, mushrooms, garlic, thyme, bay leaves, Worcestershire sauce, Guinness stout, beef stock and oregano. Add salt and pepper to taste.
4. Close the lid and cook on Low for 6 hours or on High for 3-4 hours.
5. Serve topped with parsley

Nutritional info

Calories: 235
Fats (g): 25
Net carbs (g): 5
Protein (g): 12

Broccoli Beef Soup

Servings: 4
Cooking time: 4 hours

Ingredients

    1 lb boneless beef chuck, cut into 1-inch pieces
    1 cup beef broth
    1 teaspoon sesame oil
    1 broccoli head, broke into florets
    1 garlic cloves, minced
    4 tablespoons soy sauce
    2 teaspoons brown sugar substitute
    ½ cup water
    2 tablespoons Xanthan gum

Instructions

1. Mix beef broth, sesame oil, garlic, soy sauce and sugar in a big bowl.
2. Put beef into slow cooker. Add broth mixture and mix to combine.
3. Close the lid and cook on low for 3-4 hours.

4. Mix water and Xanthan gum in a separate bow. Pour into slow cooker once the time is up.
5. Close the lid and cook on High for another 30 minutes.

Nutritional info
Calories: 370
Fats (g): 31.8
Net carbs (g): 5.3
Protein (g): 27

Superb Ground Beef Keto Style

Servings: 3
Cooking time:

Ingredients
11 oz ground beef
1 bunch kale
½ cup beef broth
2 tablespoon cayenne pepper
2 tablespoons coconut oil
1 tablespoon Chinese five spice powder
2 celery ribs, chopeed
½ onion, chopped
5 medium brown mushrooms
salt and pepper, to taste
1 cup water
2 tablespoons Xanthan gum

Instructions

1. Heat oil in a medium pan over high heat. Add ground beef and sauté for 5 minutes. Drain fat and set aside.
2. Clean the pan and heat some more oil in it, add onions and cook for 3 minutes.
3. Put beef, onions, celery ribs, mushrooms and beef broth into a slow cooker. Add cayenne pepper, Chinese five spice powder, salt and pepper to the beef and mix to combine.
4. Close the lid and cook on Low for 6 hours or on High for 4 hours.
5. Meanwhile mix water and Xanthan gum in a separate bowl. Once the beef time is up open the lid and add the mixture. Also add kale.
6. Close the lid and cook for another 30 minutes on Low.

Nutritional info

Calories: 244
Fats (g): 22.2
Net carbs (g): 6.6
Protein (g): 16.1

Broccoli and Tofu Curry

Servings: 3
Cooking Time: 4 hours

Ingredients
 1 cup firm Tofu
 6 oz light coconut milk
 1 tablespoon curry powder
 1 tablespoon Garam Masala
 1 garlic clove, minced
 ½ broccoli head, broke into florets
 ½ onion, chopped
 1 tablespoon unsweetened peanut butter

Instructions
1. Blend onion, garlic, peanut butter and coconut milk in a food processor. Add curry powder, Garam Masala, salt if needed. Mix to combine.
2. Pour the mixture into a zip lock bag and add tofu and broccoli to it. Mix and make sure tofu and broccoli are coated well.

3. Put tofu and broccoli into a slow cooker, add the sauce mixture.
4. Close the lid and cook on Low for 4 hours.

Nutritional info
Calories: 240
Fats (g): 21
Net carbs (g): 8
Protein (g): 15

Minestrone Soup

Servings: 3
Cooking time: 3-6 hours

Ingredients

  1 can black soy beans
  35 oz vegetable broth
  2 tablespoons olive oil
  ½ onion, chopped
  ½ celery, diced
  1 garlic clove, minced
  6 oz tomato paste
  2 bay leaves
  1 fresh rosemary sprig
  1 tablespoon fresh basil, chopped
  1 tablespoon fresh parsley, chopped
  1 zucchini, diced
  1 cup spinach, chopped
  salt, pepper, to taste
  parmesan cheese, grated

Instructions
1. Put beans and half of vegetable broth into a food processor and blend well.
2. Heat oil in a medium pan over high heat. Add onion, celery and garlic and cook for 15 minutes stirring constantly.
3. Pour beans and broth mixture into a slow cooker. Add remaining broth, bay leaves, paste, parmesan cheese, vegetables from the pan, salt and pepper.
4. Add rosemary, basil and parsley. Close the lid and cook on Low for 5 hours or on High for 2 hours.
5. After the time is up add zucchini and spinach. Cook for another 1 hour on Low or High.
6. Serve topped with parmesan, remove bay leaves.

Nutritional info
Calories: 304
Fats (g): 16.9
Net carbs (g): 9.9
Protein (g): 19.3

Kale Quiche

Servings: 3
Cooking Time: 3-5 hours

Ingredients

 1 cup almond milk
 6 eggs
 1 cup CarbQuick Baking Mix
 2 cups spinach, chopped
 ½ bell pepper, chopped
 3 cups fresh baby kale, chopped
 1 teaspoon garlic, chopped
 1/3 cup fresh basil, chopped
 salt, pepper, to taste
 1 tablespoon olive oil

Instructions

1. Add oil to a slow cooker or use a cooking spray.
2. Beat eggs into a slow cooker; add almond milk and CarbQuick Baking Mix, mix to combine.
3. Add spinach, bell pepper, garlic and basil, stir to combine.
4. Close the lid and cook on Low for 5 hours or on High for 3 hours.
5. Make sure the quiche is done, check the center with a toothpick, it should be dry.

Nutritional info

Calories: 273
Fats (g): 24.4
Net carbs (g): 5.8
Protein (g): 10.5

Vegan Frittata with Feta and Artichoke Hearts

Servings: 4
Cooking Time: 3 hours

Ingredients

     14 oz (1 can) artichoke hearts, drained
     12 oz (1 can) roasted red peppers, drained
     1/3 cup green onions, chopped
     8 eggs
     4 oz Feta cheese, crumbled
     salt, pepper, to taste
     ¼ cup parsley, chopped
     2 tablespoons olive oil

Instructions

1. Add oil to a slow cooker. Put artichoke hearts on the bottom, add roasted red peppers and green onions.
2. Beat eggs to combine yolks and whites well. Pour eggs into slow cooker over vegetables and stir gently.
3. Add salt and pepper, also you can add some dried thyme or rosemary. Sprinkle eggs and vegetables with Feta.
4. Close the lid and cook on Low for 2-3 hours. The cheese should melt and the eggs should be firm.
5. Serve topped with parsley.

Nutritional info

Calories: 332
Fats (g): 22.1
Net carbs (g): 8.1
Protein (g): 19.3

Spinach Stuffed Portobello

Servings: 8
Cooking time: 3 hours

Ingredients

12 oz medium sized Portobello mushrooms,
stems removed
3 tablespoons olive oil
½ onion, chopped
2 cups fresh spinach, rinsed and chopped
3 garlic cloves, minced
1 cup chicken broth
3 tablespoons parmesan cheese, grated
1/3 teaspoon dried thyme
salt, pepper, to taste

Instructions

1. Heat oil in a medium pan over high heat. Add
   onion, cook until translucent stirring
   constantly. Add spinach and thyme, cook for 1-
   2 minutes until spinach is wilted.

2. Brush each mushroom with olive oil.
3. Put 1 tablespoon of onion and spinach stuffing into each mushroom.
4. Pour chicken broth into slow cooker. Put stuffed mushrooms on the bottom.
5. Close the lid and cook on High for 3 hours.
6. Once cooked, sprinkle mushrooms with parmesan cheese and serve.

Nutritional info
Calories: 310
Fats (g): 21
Net carbs (g): 3
Protein (g): 12

Herbed Vegetable Soup

©2014 Rachel Morris

Servings: 6
Cooking time: 4-8 hours

Ingredients

½ can of 14 oz diced tomatoes
1 ½ cups vegetable broth
5 oz mushrooms, fresh or canned
1 onion, chopped
2 garlic cloves, minced
1 zucchini, thinly sliced
½ cauliflower head, broken into florets
1 teaspoon dried basil
1 packet sugar substitute
salt, pepper, to taste
1 tablespoon mozzarella cheese, grated

Instructions

1. Put tomatoes, mushrooms, onion, garlic, zucchini and cauliflower into slow cooker.
2. Add salt, pepper, basil and vegetable broth.
3. Close the lid and cook on Low for 8 hours or on High for 4 hours.
4. Serve topped with mozzarella cheese.

Nutritional info

Calories: 125
Fats (g): 15
Net carbs (g): 2.1
Protein (g): 11.9

Cauliflower Pizza with Low Carb Alfredo Sauce

Servings: 6
Cooking time: 3 hours

Ingredients

    1 head cauliflower, chopped into floret sized pieces
    2 eggs
    1 cup cheese blend (cheddar or parmesan shredded cheese blend)
    1 teaspoon dried Italian seasoning
    ½ teaspoon dried rosemary
    ¼ teaspoon salt
    4 oz homemade low carb Alfredo sauce
For sauce:
    1 oz butter, unsalted
    1 cup heavy cream
    Salt, pepper, taste
    4 oz parmesan cheese, shredded

Instructions

1. Put cauliflower florets into a food processor and blend thoroughly.
2. Put blended cauliflower into a bowl, add eggs, seasoning, salt and ¼ cheese. Mix well.
3. Add some oil into a slow cooker or use a cooking spray. Put cauliflower mixture into slow cooker and press down to form pizza base. The edges should be slightly higher around all sides.
4. To cook a low carb Alfredo Creamy Sauce, melt unsalted butter in a medium sauce pan. Add cream and stir well. Add parmesan cheese, 2 tablespoons at a time and stir constantly until incorporated. Add salt and pepper to taste, keep cooking until the sauce thickens.
5. Pour the sauce and the rest of a cheese blend onto the pizza base.
6. Close the slow cooker lid but leave a small space using a woode spoon handle.
7. Cook on High for 2-3 hours. Check if the eggs and crust are cooked well.
8. Let the pizza sit for 20-30 minutes before serving.

Nutritional info

Calories: 105
Fats (g): 5.8
Net carbs (g): 3.1
Protein (g): 7.9

Poached Salmon

Servings: 4
Cooking time: 1 hour

Ingredients
    4 medium salmon fillets
    8 oz water
    2 tablespoons dry white wine
    1 yellow onion, sliced
    ½ lemon, sliced
    ½ teaspoon salt
    ¼ teaspoon garlic powder
    ¼ teaspoon dried basil

Instructions
1. Pour water and wine into a slow cooker. Heat on High for 30 minutes with the lid open.
2. Season salmon fillets with salt, garlic powder and basil.
3. Put salmon into slow cooker. Add onion and lemon onto salmon fillets.

4. Close the lid and cook on High for 20-30 minutes.

Nutritional info
Calories: 273
Fats (g): 21
Net carbs (g): 4.2
Protein (g): 35

Cod and Vegetables

Servings: 4
Cooking time: 1-3 hours

Ingredients

4 (5-6 oz) cod fillets
1 bell pepper, sliced or chopped
1 onion, sliced
½ fresh lemon, sliced
1 zucchini, sliced
3 garlic cloves, minced
¼ cup low-sodium broth
1 teaspoon rosemary
¼ teaspoon red pepper flakes
salt, pepper, to taste

Instructions

1. Season cod fillets with salt and pepper.
2. Pour broth into slow cooker, add garlic, rosemary, bell pepper, onion and zucchini into slow cooker.
3. Put fish into your crockpot, add lemon slices on top.
4. Close the lid and cook on Low for 2-3 hours or on High for 1 hour.

Nutritional info

Calories: 150
Fats (g): 11.6
Net carbs (g): 6.2
Protein (g): 26.9

Veggie Shrimps

Servings: 3
Cooking time:

Ingredients
    1 lb raw shrimps, peeled
    2 red bell peppers, sliced
    2 green bell peppers, sliced
    ½ onion, sliced
    1 small tomato, quartered
    1 teaspoon salt
    1 teaspoon chili powder
    ½ teaspoon paprika
    ½ cup low-sodium broth

Instructions
1. Pour broth into slow cooker. Add bell peppers, tomato, onion, salt and pepper.
2. Close the lid and cook on Low for 5 hours or on High for 2 hours.
3. Season shrimps with paprika and chili powder.

4. Put shrimps into slow cooker, coat well with the broth mixture.
5. Close the lid and cook on High for 30-45 minutes.

Nutritional info
Calories: 111
Fats (g): 21.5
Net carbs (g): 4.8
Protein (g): 16.1

Fish Stock

Servings: 6
Cooking time: 4-8 hours

Ingredients

2 lb fish heads and bones, gills removed
1 tablespoon olive oil
1 onion, sliced
1 carrot, sliced
2 bay leaves
1/3 cup parsley stems
1/3 cup dill stems
2 tablespoons dry white wine
½ teaspoon rosemary
½ teaspoon dried thyme
salt, pepper, to taste
water

Instructions

1. Heat oil in a slow cooker on High. Add onion, cook until translucent stirring constantly.

71

2. Add carrot, parsley and dill stems, stir for 1 minute. Pour wine into the pan and sauté for 2 minutes.
3. Transfer the vegetables and wine mixture into a slow cooker, add fish. Add salt, pepper, rosemary and dried thyme. Pour water to cover the fish by 1 inch.
4. Close the lid and cook on Low for 6-8 hours or on High for 3-4 hours.

Nutritional info
Calories: 40
Fats (g): 11
Net carbs (g): 0
Protein (g): 5.27

Pollock Stew

Servings: 6
Cooking time: 3-5 hours

Ingredients

2 lb Pollock fillets
1 onion, chopped
3 garlic cloves, minced
1 small red chili
½ can of 14 oz diced tomatoes, not drained
¼ cup parsley, chopped
2 tablespoons olive oil
1 ½ cup water
1 tablespoon dry white wine (optional)
salt, pepper, to taste

Instructions

1. Pour oil into slow cooker, add onion, garlic, chili and parsley. Then add tomatoes (with liquid), 1 cup water and wine.

2. Close the lid and cook on Low for 5 hours or on High for 3 hours.
3. An hour before the broth is ready open the lid and add fish, ½ cup water, salt and pepper. You can add some more parsley at this step.
4. Close the lid and cook till the end.

Nutritional info
Calories: 188
Fats (g): 16.1
Net carbs (g): 3.4
Protein (g): 19.9

Trout & Broccoli Chowder

Servings: 6
Cooking time: 2 hours

Ingredients

12 oz trout fillets, skin removed
1 onion, chopped
1 tablespoon butter, unsalted
1 cup soy milk, unsweetened
1 cup water
1 package (10 oz) frozen broccoli, thawed
¼ teaspoon garlic powder
salt, pepper, to taste
1 cup cheddar cheese, shredded
1 tablespoon parsley, chopped

Instructions
1. Melt butter in a pan over high heat, add onions. Sauté for 2-3 minutes until onion softens.
2. Transfer onion to a slow cooker. Add milk, broccoli, cheese, fish, garlick powder and salt.
3. Close the lid and cook on High for 2 hours. Check if the fish is soft.
4. Serve topped with parsley.

Nutritional info
Calories: 403
Fats (g): 20.9
Net carbs (g): 6.7
Protein (g): 15.2

Garlic Shrimp

Servings: 4
Cooking time: 1 hour

Ingredients
1 lb large or jumbo shrimps, peeled
2 tablespoons butter
¼ cup olive oil
¼ tablespoon cayenne pepper
2 teaspoons paprika
4 garlic cloves, sliced
¼ teaspoon black pepper
salt, to taste
1 tablespoon parsley, chopped
1 tablespoon fresh lemon juice

Instructions
1. Add butter, oil, garlic, paprika, cayenne pepper, salt and black pepper into slow cooker. Close the lid and cook on High for 25 minutes.

2. Add shrimps to the slow cooker and stir well to coat them with oil minture.
3. Close the lid and cook on High for 30 minutes. Stir the shrimps at least once, in 10-15 minutes.
4. Serve topped with parsley and sprinkled with lemon juice.

Nutritional info
Calories: 250
Fats (g): 28.6
Net carbs (g): 2
Protein (g): 10.8

Seafood Scampi

Servings: 6
Cooking time: 1-2 hours

Ingredients
   ½ lb shrimp
   ½ lb scallops
   ½ lb mussels
   1 cup chicken broth
   2 tablespoons dry white wine
   3 tablespoons lemon juice
   2 tablespoons olive oil
   4 garlic cloves, minced
   1 tablespoon parsley, chopped
   salt, pepper, to taste

Instructions

1. Mix broth, wine, lemon juice, olive oil, garlic and parsley in a slow cooker.
2. Add shrimps, scallops and mussel, add salt and pepper, stir well to coat the seafood.
3. Close the lid and cook on Low for 2 hours or on High for 1 hour.

Nutritional info

Calories: 178
Fats (g): 16.8
Net carbs (g): 4.4
Protein (g): 20.5

Lemon Cake

Servings: 6
Cooking time:3 hours

Ingredients

1 cup coconut flour
1 cup almond flour
2 eggs
2 lemons zests
½ cup whipping cream
½ cup butter, melted
2 tablespoons butter, melted
2 teaspoons baking powder
5 tablespoons Pyure sweetner
lemon juice from 2 lemons
½ cup boiling water

Instructions

1. Mix coconut and almond flour, 2 tablespoons sweetener and baking powder in a bowl.
2. Mix eggs, ½ cup butter, whipping cream, lemon juice and lemon zest in a separate big bowl. Whisk well.
3. Add flour mixture to the egg and butter mixture and mix well until combined.
4. Line a slow cooker skillet with parchment paper. Spread the cake mixture into slow cooker.
5. Mix 3 tablespoons sweetener, boiling water, 2 tablespoons butter and 2 tablespoons lemon juice.
6. Add the topping mixture to the slow cooker over the cake base.
7. Close the lid and cook on High for 2-3 hours. Check if the cake is cooked with a toothpick. Insert it in cake center, it should come out clean.

Nutritional info

Calories: 350
Fats (g): 32.6
Net carbs (g): 10.1
Protein (g): 17.6

Low Carb Apple Bread

Servings: 6
Cooking time:3 hours

Ingredients

    2 cups almond flour
    1 tablespoon coconut flour
    ¼ cup almonds, chopped
    1 cup apple, thinly sliced
    2 eggs
    ¼ teaspoons salt
    1 teaspoon baking soda
    3 tablespoons coconut oil
    ½ teaspoon Ceylon cinnamon
    ½ cup Pyure or Swerve sweetener
    1/3 cup full fat almond or coconut milk
    1 teaspoon apple cider vinegar
    ¼ teaspoon vanilla extract

Instructions

1. Mix almond and coconut flour, cinnamon, salt, baking soda and sweetener in a big bowl.

2. Mix coconut or almond milk, coconut oil, eggs, vanilla extract and apple vinegar in a separate medium bowl.
8. Pour milk mixture into the flour mixture and mix well until combined.
3. Add apple and almonds into the bread mixture.
4. Line a slow cooker skillet with parchment paper. Spread the bread mixture into slow cooker.
5. Sprinkle some chopped almonds on top of bread.
6. Close the lid and cook on Low for 2-3 hours. Check if the bread is cooked with a toothpick. Insert it in bread center, it should come out clean.

Nutritional info
Calories: 279
Fats (g): 25.6
Net carbs (g): 3.6
Protein (g): 8.1

Chocolate Chip Zucchini Bread

Servings: 6
Cooking time: 3 hours

Ingredients

> 3 cups almond flour
> 3 eggs
> ½ cup Pyure or Swerve sweetener
> ½ cup vegetable oil
> 1 teaspoon apple cider vinegar
> 1 teaspoon baking soda
> ½ teaspoon baking powder
> 2 teaspoons Ceylon cinnamon
> ¼ teaspoon vanilla extract
> ¼ teaspoon salt
> 1 cup sugar-free chocolate chips
> 16 oz zucchini, peeled, grated

Instructions

1. Mix eggs, sweetener, vegetable oil and apple cider in a bowl.

2. Mix in flour, baking soda, baking powder, vanilla extract, cinnamon and salt. Mix well until combined.
3. Add zucchini and chocolate chips into the bread mixture.
4. Line a slow cooker skillet with parchment paper. Spread the bread mixture into slow cooker.
5. Close the lid and cook on Low for 2-3 hours. Check if the bread is cooked with a toothpick. Insert it in bread center, it should come out clean.

Nutritional info
Calories: 334
Fats (g): 47
Net carbs (g): 3.7
Protein (g): 15.1

Keto Mocha Fudge Cake

Servings: 4
Cooking time: 2-4 hours

Ingredients
2 cups almond flour
3 eggs
4 tablespoons butter, melted
¾ cup sour cream
¾ cup hot coffee
3 oz unsweetened chocolate, melted
1 teaspoon baking soda
¼ teaspoon vanilla extract
½ teaspoon salt
1 ½ cup Pyure or Swerve sweetener

Instructions
1. Mix butter and sweetener in a medium bowl. Add eggs, chocolate and sour cream, whisk well.
2. Mix in almond flour and baking soda, stir until combined.
3. Add coffee, vanilla extract and salt, mix well.

6. Grease a slow cooker with butter, line it with parchment paper. Spread the cake mixture into slow cooker.
7. Close the lid and cook on Low for 2-4 hours. Check if the cake is cooked with a toothpick. Insert it in cake center, it should come out clean.
8. Serve with whipped cream.

Nutritional info
Calories: 200
Fats (g): 18
Net carbs (g): 5.8
Protein (g): 16

Cranberry Walnut Bars

Servings: 8
Cooking time: 2-3 hours

Ingredients

12 oz cranberries, frozen or fresh
1 cup water
4.5 oz sweetener
1 tablespoon lemon juice
¼ teaspoon salt
¼ teaspoon nutmeg
2 cups almond flour
1 cup coconut, finely ground
½ cup vanilla whey protein powder
8 tablespoons salted butter, melted
¾ cup almond meal
½ cup walnuts, chopped
3 tablespoons brown sugar
3 tablespoons sugar-free chocolate chips

Instructions

1. Mix cranberries, water, 3 oz sweetener, lemon juice, salt and nutmeg in a medium pot and bring to a boil over high heat. Cook for 15 minutes until the cranberry filling thickens. Let it cool.
2. To prepare a shortbread crust, mix almond flour, coconut, protein powder, 1.5 oz sweetener, and pinch of salt in a separate bowl. Pour melted butter onto the flour mixture and mix well until clumps begin to form. Set aside a part of the mixture and save for crumb topping.
3. Line a slow cooker skillet with parchment paper. Put shortbread crust mixture into slow cooker and press down to form bars base.
4. Pour cranberry filling over the base and spread it over it. Sprinkle the walnuts, brown sugar, chocolate chips and reserved shortbread crust over cranberry filling.
5. Close the lid and cook on Low for 2-3 hours. Let cool and cut into 8 bars. Keep refrigerated.

Nutritional info

Calories: 196
Fats (g): 14
Net carbs (g): 8
Protein (g): 10

Berry Sauce

Servings: 6
Cooking time: 3 hours

Ingredients
 6 oz blackberries, fresh
 8 oz strawberries, fresh, halved
 4 oz blueberries, fresh
 ¼ cup Pyure or Swerve sweetener
 ¼ teaspoon xanthan gum (optional)

Instructions
1. Put blackberries, strawberries, blueberries and sweetener into a slow cooker.
2. Close the lid and cook on Low for 3 hours.

3. 20 minutes before the end of cooking time add xanthan gum if the sauce is not thick enough.

Nutritional info

Calories: 26
Fats (g): 11
Net carbs (g): 4.7
Protein (g): 6

Made in the USA
Middletown, DE
22 January 2018